INCANTATION
LOVE POEMS FOR BATTLE SITES

INCANTATION
LOVE POEMS FOR BATTLE SITES

XOCHITL–JULISA BERMEJO

MOUTHFEEL PRESS

Mouthfeel Press is an indie press publishing works in English and Spanish by new and established poets. We publish poetry, fiction, and non-fiction. Our books are available through our website, Amazon.com, Bookshop.org, and other online and independent booksellers, or at author's readings.

Cover Design: Cloud Cardona
Interior Design: Kimberly James, www.kimmiejwrites.com

Contact Information:

Mouthfeelbooks.com
Info.mouthfeelbooks@gmail.com

ISBN: 978-1-957840-21-5
Library of Congress Control Number: 2023944277

Published in the United States, 2023

First Printing in English
$18

MOUTHFEEL PRESS

CONTENTS

One Sweet Day: To Do List for the First Day of Spring   9

ONE

The Mermaid Game   12

Jack and Jill   14

Ursa Minor   15

Mamita, We're Going on Ahead   16

Dancing to the Tree of Their Own Mum   17

The High Dive   18

Even in War   20

The Hustle or What We Call Work   21

Birthday Candle for Breonna Taylor   23

Birth Story   25

Beach Evening Primrose   26

If La Llorona Had a Hashtag   27

Why I'll Never Again Advise Poets Against Publishing on Social Media   29

It's the 80s, Baby   31

For the Love of Home   32

TWO

Living with the Dead   37

Locating the Dead: A Protection Prayer   39

Battlefield Riddle   40

Comfort Food for White Spaces   42

Totems and Protections: WWII Days   43

Learning the Hustle or To Be a Child of Immigrants   45

Comfort Food for White Spaces   47

WARNING: No Casual Walks for Battle Sites   48

To Be American   49

Self-Portrait of Expectation   51

Comfort Food for White Spaces   53

Ghost Interview with a Soldier in the Peach Orchard   54

Counting the Dead   56

Caballito del Diablo: What Does Not Disappear   58
Comfort Food for White Spaces   60
Harvest Moon Sestina for 2017   61
Two Friends Enter a Wine Shop on Washington Street   63
Comfort Food for White Spaces   64
The Last White Man I Tried to Love   65
Battlegrounds   67

THREE

Seeking Sunday Morning Guitar Riffs   71
She Is Me, but We Are We   72
Mother Days   73
On This Page   75
The Poet's Corrido   76
Rancherita   77
I'm Not Your Torta   78
Variations on a Wooden Spoon   79
Conversation with the Heart   80
What Was Meant to Be   81
The Way Men Use Me   83
Sanctuary   85
Ritual of Wholeness   86

NOTES ON POEMS   89
PAGES 29-30 ENDNOTES   92
ACKNOWLEDGEMENTS   94
AUTHOR'S BIOGRAPHY   97

INCANTATION
LOVE POEMS FOR BATTLE SITES

One Sweet Day: To Do List for the First Day of Spring

San Gabriel, March 2017

Rise and feed the cat staring you down from her corner of the bed. One scoop of food, one drag of water, and then back to blankets.

Place head on pillow and try to recall if you dreamed last night. Try to recall if dream was nightmare, if nightmare was memory masquerading as dream.

Listen to the helicopters circling above. Let the sound continue to confuse wake and dream, reality and nightmare.

See the cat happily return to bed, now well-fed. Welcome the warmth of her body snuggled up against an arm.

Consider rising. Consider reading. Consider walking. Consider the helicopters, still circling.

Answer the phone call from your mother: "There was a shooting at the Temple City sheriff station." Oblige her command: "Stay inside."

Rise a second time to make coffee, answer emails, grade. Google "Temple City shooting." Attempt to visualize invisible city lines separating there from here.

Read the text from your 11-year-old nephew: "Stay home there was a shooting near our home and my school." And the next: "Take chewy inside pleas."

Call the dog in from the yard and listen to him scratch at the door to be let back out. Watch the dog and cat stare each other down through a plastic gate.

Try to ignore the incessant circling both outside and in.

Take a breath to push away creeping anxiety. Remember an article that said to make the bed, clean the house, take a walk. Remember that you cannot take a walk.

In the kitchen, wash dishes, wipe down the counter. In the bathroom, scoop out the litter, replace the roll of toilet paper. Do this while listening to Mariah Carey songs.

Notice the absence of helicopters and decide it's your turn to leave. Grab a bag, tie sneakers, and head for the street.

Smell perfumed air heavy with loquats. Pick a yellow berry and bite its tart meat. Feel the sticky juice between your fingers.

Begin again.

ONE

"The children must play, even in war."

–Alma Luz Villanueva, "Violation"

The Mermaid Game

"We are learning and re-learning how to honor each other, how to go deep, how to take turns, how to find nourishing light again and again."

- Alexis Pauline Grumbs, Undrowned

If I were a mermaid, my tail would sparkle
pink and the shells covering perky breasts,
tart yellow. I would be forever summer
like ice cream trucks and cherry slush,
like two kids naïvely turning crisp
under the shallows of a three-foot pool.
In the ocean, I'd swim spin, full body
blowing bubbles. I'd dive below weight
of water to speak secrets only meant
for you—blue lips shaping, *Ah wa wu*—
and together we'd lap circles building
whirlpools, inviting rainbow fish
to catch a ride. And not until I tired, drifted
to the sea floor, laid my body across a rock,
heard you say, *I love you, too,*
could I dream of the undrowned
children never aged. Brown, big-headed

by octopus, all the while being protected
by whales and dolphins in a way that said
they were always safe. And when I'd wake,
I'd feed myself pineapple, do my stretches,
squid ink dreams on paper making them real
enough to be true, and tail to the surface to find
you bathed in sunlight and us, ready to go again.

Jack and Jill

For Hazel & the UTLA Teachers, April 23, 2020

If the farthest I travel from you
is the closest I come to nature,
then distance is a blessing,

time a balloon, love a wetland.
I admire a lizard scurrying into
brush, listen for mourning doves

asking, "Who?" I'm reminded of you
dancing in red polka dots against
the rain, how red-winged teachers

fought brackish conditions together
calling, "NOW!" And the children
race up the hill, as children do.

Ursa Minor

For Carlos Hernández Vázquez, 16
For Juan de León Gutiérrez, 16
For Felipe Gómez Alonzo, 8
For Jakelin Caal Maquin, 7
For Wilmer Josué Ramírez Vásquez, 2
For Angie Valeria Martínez, 23 months
For Mariee Juárez, 19 months

Each star belongs to a galaxy we can't identify
with the naked eye. Download the app
to hold the unseen in your hands.

Star registries, like the Sonoran Desert,
have searchable maps. Somewhere a 16-year-old
names a star for a first love. An eight-year-old

follows the northern star like a beacon.
A seven-year-old sings a rhyme. And the babies?
Well, the babies are goo-gee-gawing, but their mothers

know those wet, fleshy mouths mean *estrella*.
In the sky a little bear plays in a river of stars,
but on the land red dots mark the dead.

Over the bodies lay hands. Over the bones
pour dirt. Over the rotting country
watches a seven-point constellation.

Mamita, We're Going on Ahead

For Claudia Patricia Gómez González

Mamita, you would've been proud
to see your princesita pushing
against current to cross the Río Bravo.

But when feet reached the shore,
orders came to hide. I did my best
to make my body soft as sand.

It wasn't enough. Only a mile in
and minutes on the land, border patrol
shot me. Long grasses held me.

I thanked earth for its kindness.
With my face half in blood, half in dirt,
I heard a woman screaming.

She named me *chava, ruca, muchacha*.
I wished to thank her, too, but reeds
wrapped around my ears. Sang me to sleep.

Mamita, don't cry. I've gone on ahead.
One day, we'll be reunited, but my blood stays,
soaks the soil, stains their precious border.

Dancing to the Tree of Their Own Mum

For Maggie & Georgia, April 9, 2020

You're a boogie down Bonsai
when the music goes, *Get down!*
Get down! How might it feel
to be a leopard cuff, tiger heart,
starlight lapel? Shake a log, girl!
You're so bright, you gotta squinch.

Daughter shrub grooves beside you.
She throws up arms & shouts, *Yeah, man!*
You root her on, *What's that now?*
She howls again, *Yeah, man!*
Yeah, man! you call back and forth
like a marvel. Trunks quake

as mothers & daughters orchestrate
a sunny day despite the storm.

The High Dive

When I see my nephew's sun and chlorine-bleached hair smoothly gelled like a
gentleman, pompadour cresting in a ducktail, his mother shaking her head at his
refusal to use the damage control shampoo she purchased, "Won't even shower,"
she says to which he

shrugs, "I'll just
get dirty again,"
when I think
of his hair
as a badge
of pride earned
lapping lanes,
prepubescent
limbs cutting
water, growing
stronger,
more man
with each stroke,
I'm reminded
of the pools
of Lake Chapala,
and how he
flooded gates

no hesitation,

flew so fast

I nearly missed

the chance to

raise my phone

— SNAP! —

flung body before

the blue below.

Even in War

For Gabrielito, April 22, 2020

My dearest, won't you
turn away from the flickering
screen, so we can talk?
What have I told you
about games with guns?
No. No, you're right.
That's not what I came
to say. Let me begin again.
Remember when
I cradled you small
and squishy in my arms?
Of course, you wouldn't,
but your scrunched-up-face
once slept against my chest
all the same. My heart
knows you. Tall as a building
without a corner. Here. Stay
in this crook I call a home. Be
a child a while longer. Show me
your game. I promise to play.

The Hustle or What We Call Work

"Mr. [Andrés] Guardado was not wearing a security uniform or clothing nor wearing any type of gun belt. He was not yet 21 years old therefore he was unable to be legally employed as an armed security guard. There is no record of Mr. Guardado possessing a security license."

- Los Angeles Sheriff's Commander Chris Marks, August 12, 2020

Andrés is my brother's name. His son, Mando, is 13. In five years Mando will be the same age as Andrés when he was shot in the back by Compton cops. At 18, Mando will still be Andrés's son. Still be my nephew. Still be new, and not, yet, a man. At 15, my dad was employed at a pharmacy. It was his first job in the States. He made deliveries like the kid in *It's a Wonderful Life*. Like George Bailey, my dad always had to be a man

Andrés is my brother. Andrés is my dad. Andrés is my dad's brothers, too.

My uncle has a 44-year-old silkscreen business. Probably the oldest, longest-owned silkscreen business by a Mexican immigrant in all Los Angeles, maybe California, maybe even the USA. Why not? Beyond rows and rows of dusty, wooden-framed screens, this story is the record.

Starting in the 1970s my uncle employed his dad until he died of lung cancer in 1994. Brothers, sons, nephews, and cousins from Mexico all worked at designing logos and pressing tees. They are Andrés, too. Today, as women often do, his daughter does her best to order the front office.

One hot day in July 1999, my uncle asked if I wanted to earn extra money. Nineteen and home for the summer, a gray van I'd never seen waited outside. Not knowing the job or uniform, I threw on orange shorts and a ribbed, striped tank.

Jumping in the van, I found his son driving and my uncle riding shotgun.

On a shaded street in the perimeter of the Rose Bowl, I stood at a T in the road with shirts slung over a shoulder. I held one open to oncoming cars so they could see the World Cup design. No licenses for logos. No permits to sell.

When a cop rolled by my cousin ordered me back in the van and drove us to a new spot. "Is this illegal?" Only a look for my dumb question.

When I hadn't sold a thing, my uncle said I could forget it. Free of t-shirts, I followed blaring horns to the *Save Ferris* concert happening across the lawns. Kicking my feet to a song, my uncle strolled up with two scalped tickets, and said let's go. That's how I witnessed live the winning penalty kick and Brandi Chastain ripping off her uniform, bearing a black sports bra to the world.

To my knowledge, no one died that day though many did things we were told we were unable to do.

Birthday Candle for Breonna Taylor

June 5, 2020

I wish to gift you a late sunset
on a cool June night, cicada
chirping as you stride into the street

in a bomb black dress
that hugs curves just right,
and you feeling fine.

Accessories glint, and your man
holds the car door open, ready
to escort you to any place you say.

Red restaurant serving
tiny bits of tartar paired
with Argentinian wine.

Side door speakeasy pouring
jazz and honey over
a single-sweat slab of ice.

Club spinning dancehall
while multicolored moons orbit
your goddess body. And you spin

lush living until muscles
say stretch, and you
rest. And then, you

                         wake.

Birth Story

For Mom, April 28, 2020

The story goes, you always wanted a daughter, but never liked the name Xochitl. It took three baby boys before you could finally thank the universe for the flower that bloomed from your earth. The story goes, you pained for a week. "Rubén!" you screamed to a husband in the middle of the night. At the hospital, doctors shook heads. Said, "Go home. Wait." But they didn't know you never stilled. Instead, you had a husband take you for a Sunday drive up a mountain. Found a spring creek. Nine months big, you balanced over stones and babbling water. Had the baby within asked for a drink? Did you know a flower needed the shade of trees, the sweet talk of river to call her home? No, the story is the mountain knew you. Had requested you come.

Beach Evening Primrose

For Óscar Alberto Martínez Ramírez & Angie Valeria Martínez

Blanket the banks
of the River Grande in gold
flowers with hearts
for petals. Pick petals
one by one. Chant:
*He loves me. He loves me
not.* Braid and knot
stems into wreaths. Toss them
into water. Watch them
buoy.

Lay petals in paths
for little girls to skip
back and forth across water.
Dazzle the desert in yellow.
Confuse ground for butterfly
sky, so eyes trained
on borders fumble up
and down, north and south.
En todos lados, let wings
blossom.

If La Llorona Had a Hashtag

If she had been very quiet
no one would know her.
The story would be no story,
just as there is no name.

If La Llorona had a hashtag
it might be #mishijos,
or #remembermishijos,
or #somosamoreterno.

Then maybe citizens
might question
how her children drowned
and by whose hands.

Because if I know anything,
it wasn't by her own.
History teaches me
the guilty like their laws

so the guilty can sleep well
and the guilty feel just

in their beds, in their homes,
in their city lines, and maps.

But the guilty don't cry,
even as they say, "Thoughts
& Prayers," for our babies
born open water.

Why I'll Never Again Advise Poets Against Publishing on Social Media[1]

Because Elijah McClain was just going home.

Because Breonna Taylor was just resting and watching a movie with her boyfriend at home.

Because Dominique Rem'mie Fells dared to love her body adorned in art like a home.

Because George Floyd called out for his momma.

Because Ma'Khia Bryant first called her grandmother.

Because Andrés Guardado is called a man in news reports, but he was working his way to becoming one.

Because over 1,125,366[2] people have died of Covid in the US, and people still call it just the flu.

Because Carlos Gregorio Hernández Vásquez died of the flu on a concrete floor with only foil blankets to comfort him.

Because Toyin Salau shouldn't have needed refuge.

Because Vanessa Guillén shouldn't have needed rescue.

Because Óscar Alberto Martínez Ramírez and his daughter, Angie Valeria, shouldn't have needed to risk it.

Because Sandra Bland didn't kill herself.[3]

Because Tȟuŋkášila Šákpe is stolen Lakota land and four presidents make a desecration.[4]

Because the Standing Rock still fight to protect clean water.[5]

Because Flint still waits for clean water.[6]

Because government paid ads say to wear masks and wash hands, but with what water?

Because for some, words can't ever be washed clean enough to be heard.

Because Elijah McClain said, "That's my house. I was just going home."

It's the 80s, Baby

For Ryane, April 5, 2020

You kick back,
Ebony opened
on your lap,
Keds on a futon
chair, not one care.
Rudy Huxtable & you
beam like besties.
Show me how
to unlock retro bliss,
to blow away today's blues
with dandelion wishes.
You once told me
your eyes
are always shut
in photos.
You said it
like steamed broccoli,
but your eyes
are cotton candy,
and this is no rainy day.
Sweets, ask eyes
to spin kinder futures:
us again
together.

For the Love of Home

San Gabriel, July 2020

I

May this poem honor
the Tongva people.
May morning steps
with mom reclaim
the corner of Live Oak
& a street named
for a conqueror
I refuse space to
with bougainvillea's
resolve to topple
a wooden wall.
May these lines relieve
Toypurina of her post.

II

When alarms announce
curfews and police
attempt to stomp
the people's demands,
Dad advises Mission Glass
at Cesar Chavez for replacing
a cracked windshield,
but nothing delivers
a Black father safely home

to his daughter.
San Gabriel Mission's
thatched roof catches fire
at 4am testing structure,
but nothing suffices.
When a priest stamps ash
to foreheads he says,
"Remember you are dust."

III

Fire is renewal. Land
cannot forget. Land
is mother. Mother's womb
is structure. Ash
is not nothing. Futures
are sketched in ash.

IV

When the bells finally came down
their tongues were fat from centuries
of wagging. Being lashed to ropes
and forced to cry was not the life
they dreamed when first molded, but now
they sing as 262 copper hearts, one
for every year the mission stood.
The Indigenous Women's Monument,
forged by Native craftspeople,
sanctified art installation,
is "Dedicated in the year 2033
by the people of the City of San Gabriel
as a place for healing," reads the sign
in five languages. Not far off

a concrete pedestal remains
from a vote to discard the statue.
Girls from the high school,
volunteers baptized "Green Skirts,"
hauled the bronze to South El Monte
and dumped it into the river marshes.
Army of Engineers ordered, "Let it drown,"
and the blue herons keep guard.
Come. Sit in this circle. Listen
to the women. Be touched by medicine.

TWO

"And yet, death keeps us watching."

–Cherríe Moraga, *Loving in the War Years*

Living with the Dead

After 11th Massachusetts Infantry Monument, Gettysburg National Military Park

A ghost yanks at my feet
dragging me from navy sheets
and onto the floor. I fumble
for the phone, my hand asleep.
I'm pregnant, I say.
The baby is yours. Tingling fingers
speak to what's real and not.

It's pitch black, and yet, I feel
the line of teal cannons
below my second-story window
watching. In the living room,
a battle flag set in a field of white,
hate on display, taunts. I never
turn out the lights.

The land is so dark, I doubt
the day. At dawn, I rush out
barefoot to meet the sun
and name the fog. Down the lane
a single hand rises from concrete
clutching a saber. The hand thrusts
into the air like the living dead.

Well, all ends that is well, the hand
thinks, but thoughts choke

on stone and stumble. The hand
hacks before trying again:
Well ends well. That's all.
And again: *Well, well, all's that ends.*
No, the thought is simply, *All ends.*

Locating the Dead: A Protection Prayer

Klingel House, GNMP

Ubalda Durán Bermejo, guide me
through this hallowed place. Help me
keep judgment keen and body safe.
Wrap me in an arm, and with lips
puckered and eyes on face, suspend me
in that space before the kiss.

Grandma, this is to say thank you
for winged blessing, chirping grass,
soft moss fixed to stonewalls.
I survey grounds alone with nothing
but my brown skin to offer. This is how
I attend to what's buried in your name.

GNMP

Battlefield Riddle

This poem is riddled
with monuments;

men on alert,
men on horses,
men on stomachs
aiming for a shot,

ones with men
holding flags,
& ones with
no men at all:

column,

obelisk,

tower.

Where is final breath,
mother's waiting,
gravedigger's sweat?

Country treated with concrete
keeps out light. Cannot hallow.

The wind, the wind
jostles yellow leaves
from trees, and yet,
monuments are still,
preserved in position:

        right
            flank
                sealed
                    to bolder,

left flank
nestled
in wheat.

Peach trees die and are replanted
again and again. When is a man—
feet posed, eyes pointed, fingers poised—

        forgiven weapon,

                welcomed earth?

Comfort Food for White Spaces

It's my first Saturday in Gettysburg, and down the lane at Eisenhower's Homestead is the annual WWII Days living history encampment. Kate, a friend, drove me here from Virginia and is staying the night. Into pinup fashion, she marvels at 1940s collectibles and talks about an Italian grandfather who piloted in the war. I mark every white man I pass and think about Navajo code talkers and Mexican foot soldiers. I find one ally, a man in a Tuskegee Airman uniform. He smiles wide and offers a tour of his tent. I want to ask him questions, but don't.

That night, Kate and I attend the USO dance. She's a bombshell in a jungle-print strapless dress with a sweetheart neckline. I'm Rosie the Riveter in denim overalls and a polka dot headscarf. Kate dances with a handsome salt-and-pepper soldier in uniform. On the third song she insists he dance with me. Playing the friend, I dutifully allow him to spin me out and reel me in. As we move, he confides he's married and a father. After another spin, I learn of his 30-year-old daughter and eight-year-old grandson. I look him in the face seeking his age, and then, as he walks off the dance floor, a slight limp.

"Why do people want to remember war like this?" I ask Kate as we leave the dance. "You think we shouldn't?" she seethes. "Are you saying Hitler shouldn't be hated?"

This is not what I'm saying.

Still early, I *Yelp* the closest bar and navigate us to an Irish pub. "You wanna go in there?" Kate points to brick façade and gas lamps. "You'll ask more questions and get your ass kicked." Back at Klingel Farm, I text Andy in California and tell him I miss how he lets me think out loud.

In the morning, before Kate starts her three-hour drive home, we toast yellow Eggo waffles in the shape of Frisbees and release hurt into the air. Once alone, I launch myself into a search for the Tuskegee Airman, or a place for questions.

Totems and Protections: WWII Days

After a conversation with the Tuskegee Airman

Little red bibles fixed to fit a palm
sit in a stack with the sign:
TAKE ONE.

Hold bible to ear to hear
prayers. Soldier's desire for home
sounds like waves;

a grave. What object
keeps him alive?
Or is it a lie?

Must the object be close to skin
to understand shirt
or shirt pin?

Boot grasps foot when remembering
the trembling of tanks.
Spectacles reflect

wings of B-52 bombers, but what
holds the shattered bodies,
the children's shock?

Pen remembers men's longing,
but does stretcher remember
its embrace of Death?

Photo captures soldiers in a field of mud
waiting on over-turned helmets
for the word of God.

Place helmet on head. Cover
ears. See how we listen
and don't.

Learning the Hustle or To Be a Child of Immigrants

TGIF plays in the background.
Tanner's in the kitchen,
while you and your brother
work the living room floor
assembly line. Individually package
merchandise: slip metallic decals
in the shape of cowboy hats
into cellophane envelopes,
crease the flap, staple it shut.
Fold multicolored bandanas.
Stack them by state—Durango,
Jalisco, Chihuahua, Nayarit.
Saturday morning, wake early.
No cartoons. Pack the van.
Saturday afternoon, display inventory.
Saturday evening, watch men
in 501s, bandanas wagging
from back pockets, dance
with one leg propelling. Gritos
bounce off the Budweiser-soaked
ground, bodies move like broken,
crowds build like fire. Try your best
to not be frightened. Sell
what you can. Parrot your mother,
the way she flirts. "¡Ándale caballero!"
They laugh. She pockets the cash.
Remember your great-grandfather
sold raspados in the church square

with syrups concocted from scratch.
Remember your grandfather
constructed a rascuache barbershop
behind his Boyle Heights home
furnished with an authentic barber chair,
white porcelain and smooth.
Remember your father
drove you on afternoon turnarounds
to Tijuana for new stock
in a brown Volkswagen van.
Hot, beige vinyl stuck to your thighs.
Across the border, cousins manning
a taco shop didn't speak your language,
skinned goats hung hooked
from the kitchen ceiling, pink chicle
became the payment for a day's work.

Comfort Food for White Spaces

It's Monday morning, and I'm touring the battlefields with Bonnie, a woman in her 50s or 60s with short blond hair. She's a poet, too. "So we understand each other," she says. "What can you tell me about the Black soldiers?" I ask. "Oh, there weren't any. It was illegal." She stops the van next to an apple orchard. "Look at the way the trees bend like they're dancing. Now, that's a poem." She waits for me to note her words.

Bonnie drives us down Confederate Avenue in a white van. She directs me to admire southern state monuments as they pass. At Florida she stops and reads: "They fought with COURAGE and DEVOTION for their IDEALS." She places a hand at her chest and slows her speech for the final words: "They enable us to meet with confidence any sacrifice which confronts US AS   AMERICANS."

I'm silent.

Back at Klingel Farm, the image of a re-enactor waving a Confederate flag in front of the Virginia Monument pulls at my thoughts like an ocean current. Later tonight, I'll call Andy for a tether, but he'll only tell me to go to sleep.

For lunch, I make a sandwich out of Buddig Honey Roasted Turkey and sit under the shade of a white oak to eat. Tourists in a horse-drawn buggy watch me as display. I bite into the pink meat. Let it slide down my throat.

WARNING: No Casual Walks for Battle Sites

GNMP

Off Sickles Ave, I boot across wet grass
bound for the Peach Orchard.
Beyond a yellow field, I mark
an older couple navigating
a blue motorcycle. White hairs escape
from under distinctly red caps. *Great!*
At a five-pillar stone monument
observing positions and statistics, I break.
Glance back. From her position
atop an idling bike, the woman aims
a camera in my direction and shoots.
Below the rim of my straw hat, sweat
multiplies across battle lines.

Advancing up a tree-lined bend, I reach
a lookout of Little Round Top. I spy
a semi-circle of ivory markers guarding
some old skirmish. A man heavy
on his hog blocks the road and my path.
His wide, white mustache bristles
in the wind. I face him in the sunglasses,
gulp doubt, say, "Hello."
He scans my body. I brace myself.
He scans my brown body
and shudders as if to say I'm ugly.
He mouths a fat "NO," and I know
I'm in enemy territory. He fires his engine.

To Be American

Dad works in Spanish radio promotions,
stations with a crew of twenty-somethings
in supermarket parking lots, soccer game
tailgates, county fair concessions,
and music festival midways, wakes at 3am
for a Rose Parade post, stays out till 3am
for a Coliseum assignment.
I tell him, "Wear a jacket."
For Christmas, I bought him a bomber
with plenty of lining. From the field,

Dad sends videos over WhatsApp:
Maná in a studio, an old corrido about love,
a newscaster making a joke in Spanish
I don't understand. —Reader, have you
fake-laughed at a joke hoping to pass
knowing your face floods confusion.—

Dad disburses key chains, coffee mugs,
ballpoint pens, and baseball caps. Freebies
stamped with Jarritos, Cornflakes, K-Love,
and Corona logos. Items supply family
drawers and cabinets. On the ground,
between parked cars and sliding doors,

Dad takes fire. "Get that Mexican
music out of here!" In Orange County
a person kicked over his equipment.
"Go home! Go back to Mexico!"

Dad served me Sunday morning eggs
with this latest story. They don't know

Dad got drafted, reported for duty, waved bye
to Boyle Heights and headed for boot camp.
Once assigned to an engineering unit,

Dad toured DC, then New York City
during the 1964 World's Fair. I wondered
what wonders he saw, but he said,
"I didn't have any money." Back at base,

Dad waited for deployment, kept supplies
in order and his gun clean. "They tried
to brainwash us," he told me,
"but they didn't speak my language."

Dad traveled back to L.A. on leave,
boarded a bus for the border,
and then another for Guadalajara.
Sheltered with a childhood friend.
Young and single in the city, I imagined
him partying and picking up girls.
"I mainly kept to myself," he said. But never
how lonely it can be "waiting for home."

Self-Portrait of Expectation

After Chen Chen

A poet seated at a desk catches dream details
on paper while morning widens in the window.
Just outside that window, a line of teal cannons
follows a country road. On the desk, a library
of poets and a framed photo of her grandma look on.
Isn't it picturesque? See how she is a beautiful thing.

A poet alone in a haunted house, bloodshot
and crazed to finally find the dawn. Below her,
on the first floor, the second official Confederacy flag
—battle flag set in a field of white—stands stuck
in a vase. A small novelty item, it decorates
the living room mantel with the "Stars and Stripes."

For five days she tells herself lies she knows
are lies. Morning of the sixth, she rolls up the white
between fingers like a cigarette, drops it
into a nearby pot, slides it into a cabinet,
and shuts the door. *This isn't history,*
she thinks, *this is now, and I have failed.*

From then on, she asks Confederate ghosts not
to shove her when descending the stairs. She raises
a hand to the air and pleads, "Please don't, Rogelio."
She gives the ghost a name. She builds art about being
alone: a strong, brave woman, look how she explores
the world with a brilliant smile; see a woman

good at selfies. She wants to meet expectation,
but tonight she can't help being a girl heartbroken
over a boy fretting with plastic covers and pricings
in a Pasadena record shop with a flask of gin to his lips.
Though she tells him she is sad and bruised,
he cannot understand, and worse, he does not care.

A picture of loneliness, she begins to sink below
floorboards to where it's said two Confederates' bodies
were found. Before she's swallowed, her father calls.
"I wanted to hear your voice," he says.
She insists she's fine. So much inspiration! She forgets
he was the one who taught her to name fears.

Comfort Food for White Spaces

Wednesday evening Andy texts: "Can't chat tonight. I have a date. The shop's slow if you want to talk now."

It's dusk, and I'm in the Peach Orchard conducting an interview with a ghost. The sun has hit the tree line, and the smokey quartz I hold catches the light. My hand shakes. My mouth curls. I tell myself not to react. I pack up everything and ride back to Klingel. I lug the bike inside, kick off my shoes, drink a glass of water, take a seat in the living room, and give him a call.

"Hey there," he says, cheery and everyday. He talks about records and customers. When he pauses, I tell him I'm upset. "Oh, you're just mad because I have a date," he says. "No, I'm mad because we had a date, and you're canceling," I say. "Fine. I'm sorry," he says through gritted teeth like a child. Our conversation continues. He tells me a story from his day. I walk into the kitchen because I want to be doing anything but this. I don't hear his words. The story he tells will never be recalled.

I interrupt: "So you're over this then?" I ask him to be clear with me. I hear his voice circle. "I don't think we're meant to be," he finally says. "OK, well, talk to you— " How does one finish a conversation like this? "Bye," I say and hang up.

The next day I buy a can of SpaghettiOs and warm the thick lava syrup on the stove. The Os are different sizes and swim in space like planets or realities. What might it be like to jump in?

Ghost Interview with a Soldier in the Peach Orchard

After Ghostlines Collective

Dried peach pits litter the ground reminding me of bones.
Are your bones below the soil? Is this why you care
for fields dressed in morning fog snagging on fences?

How do you want to be remembered? If you could
write anything on one of these monuments
flanking the orchard, what would you write?

Have you ever pledged allegiance to a flag, any flag?
Have you ever loved a flag like your mother's arms?
Speaking of your mother's arms, how did they smell

when tucked tight below your nose?
Like fresh baked loaves or maybe stone?
I want a better simile, but I need you to tell me.

If you could go back, what would you say
to your father? What would you teach your daughter?
I still hope to have a child, so consider this advice.

In your final moments, whom did you think of?
Did you write this someone love letters home
with sign-offs like *I wait to hold you* and *Forever yours*?

I sit below a tree alone at twilight because I'm always alone
and afraid. Are you here with me? Is that you rustling
the branches? I tell you, I'm done being afraid.

Do you hate war? Did you ever love war?
Am I totally off and is War like God, unknown,
all around, a mystery too big to understand?

I want to believe in love like some believe in god.
Will you help me? Do you think I'm crazy?
Do you think I'm beautiful? Would you date me?

Don't answer that. What can I say?
I talk too much when I'm anxious. Please tell me
a question exists that will help us both let go.

Counting the Dead

1,000.
        10,000.
                50,000.

Official numbers
        casually change
                when not all

casualties count.
        Dumb ass bitch!
                Dumb ass bitch!

Dumb ass bitch!
        I chant myself
                awake. The dream:

a blond woman
        wearing a crown
                calls me white.

I snatch
        the crown
                off her head.

This anger
        has no place
                to go

except
        to grind teeth
                into dust,

a stone jaw
     made square
         for grinding.

I check
     Facebook.
         50 people killed

in Vegas.
     I imagine
         each one

standing
     in a field
         of wheat.

Caballito del Diablo: What Does Not Disappear

After Sara Uribe

yellow leaves

swirl

counterclockwise

in a field

dancing devil made of dust

crops chopped

land lost

land back

dirt replaces

golden glow

the unnamed

and numbered

run amok

frenzied leaves

scatter

fall

quiet

captures
green iridescence
a vortex

How do I love you?

listen

trill in trees

crickets

never

stop

singing

Comfort Food for White Spaces

It's my last full day in Gettysburg, and I join a ranger talk in the cemetery. I want to hear something about Lincoln. I want to hear something with goodness, but the ranger leads us down the middle of a long corridor of trees to illustrate Victorian aesthetics. For an hour, he lectures on white ideals, white status, white beauty. Finally, he finishes by reciting the Gettysburg Address and gives himself chills. Before he walks away, I ask, "Where did Lincoln speak?" He looks around. "We don't really know." He points to a tiny angel atop a tombstone behind the iron bars of a fence. "We think somewhere about there," he says and walks away. As I return to my bike, I pass at least 10 small stone and cement monuments perfectly marking each brigade's position and steps. I stop at a Dairy Queen, buy a soft-serve chocolate fudge sundae with nuts, and scoop the sugar with a red spoon. Smooth it over my tongue.

Harvest Moon Sestina for 2017

My father cleaned the nopales of needles.
"It's too hard," he said, his fingers full
of cuts. Tonight, I'm alone in a farmhouse in fall,
but this happened in spring among blossoms
and birthdays. This is how he says, "Love,
I want to see you smile." All day the cacophony

of news from the chump, that bum, his cacophony
of lies and hate creates a feeling in me like a needle
scratching across vinyl. Each morning I rise full
of omens, esophagus gagging on the sun. The fall
is coming. I soothe an acid belly with pink blossoms,
red wine, and strange men. I call each one love

and insist on being spooned. One I tried to love
so hard, I happily worshipped his cacophony
of shortcomings. I wanted to make a bent needle
point north. I wanted to know two people full
of sharp corners could fit flush, but he refused to fall
into the arms I held open for him like a blossom.

If I were vindictive, I would curse gin blossoms
upon his giant, drunk nose, but I'm too lovely.
That's a lie. I'm too scared. A cacophony
of fears rattle in my head like ghosts. They needle
me in my sleep manifesting in nightmares full
of me screaming in people's faces. Eyes fall

disgusted on a target before the tongue drops. Fallout
is the waking realization ugliness blossoms
in me. Fear can birth monsters, but I will love
this self despite myself. I will quiet the cacophony
by turning the dial, pushing the needle
slightly to the left. Slowly, I will become so full

of joy, I won't remember how it is to have a belly full
of doubts drowning in cheap cabernet. I will fall
in love with me. I will nurse my heart until it blossoms
into a blood Dahlia. Each petal will say, "She loves
me." I will pull petal after petal to hear their cacophony
and hope one day to feel it like medicine from a needle.

Nopal needles scratch the skin leaving hands full
of marks more beautiful than blossoms. Pennsylvania fall
is a cacophony in yellow. I whisper, "Hold on, love."

Two Friends Enter a Wine Shop on Washington Street

You don't belong, greets a scoff like a bell as they push through the door. The Thai-American woman—visiting for the night from Manhattan—doesn't hear, but the Mexican-American woman, even with her back turned, does. She finds the scoff standing behind a tasting counter.

"Excuse me?" she asks.

The scoff blinks.

"Did I miss something?"

"Oh, um. I was just wondering if, hmmm. Do you need help?" The scoff's voice is unsurprisingly unimpressive.

"My friend and I are looking for a bottle to go with dinner."

The scoff rolls its eyes.

The Mexican-American woman squares her feet eye to eye. *Do you see me? I see you. I. See. You.*

They walk out and buy cider from a shop down the street.

Fuck the scoffs.

***

In Clovis, California, a shotgun greeted me as I explored rolling ranch hills, research for a still unfinished novel.

You don't belong, said the shotgun. This was the sum of the conversation.

Fuck the shotguns, too.

Comfort Food for White Spaces

It's close to 5pm when I bike to the post office with a backpack full of poetry books. *Antígona González*, *There Are More Beautiful Things Than Beyoncé*, *When I Grow Up I Want to Be a List of Further Possibilities*, and *Unaccompanied* have become my company. I'm mailing my comrades home instead of lugging them across the country on my back. I wobble from foot to foot trying to decide on the packaging. The woman behind the counter doesn't ask if I need help. She doesn't look me in the eyes. The post office is ready to close, and my bike is taking up the entranceway. There is no bike rack outside. I choose a package size and fill the empty spaces between books with notes from my research and pages torn out of my dream journal. On the label, I write "San Gabriel, California" for "To." And then "San Gabriel, California" for "From." I get the feeling I'm spinning in space until I hand over my money.

"I'm sending this package home," I tell her. "Oh, that's good," she says without inflection. In my head I hear, *Good. Go home.* These books will arrive before me. They will be welcomed into my home and sat at the kitchen table. They will smell longaniza sizzling in a pan on the stove. Their pages like tongues will crave the salty content spooned over a fried egg. Tortillas, beans, and coffee with a stick of cinnamon will seep into their poems. *Go home,* I tell myself. No one waits for you to stay.

The Last White Man I Tried to Love

I called the cocktails he mixed, the cigarettes he rolled,
the steak dinners he treated me to reparations
and did my best to ignore the fact we only drank gin
even though he knew I preferred whiskey,
or that we went for sushi only when I insisted.

In the evenings, he sat in his armchair with me at his side
on the couch as we read from separate books. "You fit right
into my life," he said lifting a pointed nose from pages.
Later, that nose buried between my legs as he studied my lips,
sucked on my swells until I came loud. "Good girl," he said.

One night, I read him a passage aloud from *Loving
in the War Years* about women like me needing attention
and care. (I did not read what it said about men like him.)
"And don't I care for you?" he asked. "Yes," I said
knowing the real answer, he probably didn't care to hear.

Once he set me up in his office with a fresh martini,
and left me alone to write. Later, he brought me a plate
of heated frozen lasagna and said, "I like you in my space."
That night, my clothes stayed on. I went home early
for a job the next day, and I was thrilled by all of this.

But then he started playing records just for himself
by 20th-century white men seeking island fantasy and flavor.
When I asked, "What are you listening to?" he said, "Exotica."
I heard *erotica.* "It sounds pretty fetishy to me," I said,
but he didn't get it. He never did. I didn't get any that night.

And when I brought him a square of tres leches cake
and a mango chile lollipop, leftovers from a family party
he had no intention of attending, and didn't try either,
I wasn't surprised. Still, I didn't stop offering him
all of me, and he didn't stop taking only what he liked.

Battlegrounds

GNMP

Motorcycles and white tour vans speed
between behemoth granite shafts, shove
my body by their force, leave me roadside
and wandering fields. Little is funny
when you're Chicana and walking
a Civil War site not meant for walking.
Regardless, I ask park rangers and guides
for stories on Mexicans soldiers.

Receive shrugs. No evidence in statues
or statistics. In the cemetery, not one
Spanish name. I'm alone in the giftshop.
It's the same in the post office, the market,
the antique shop with KKK books on display.
In the peach orchard, I prepare a séance,
sit cross-legged in grass and hold
a smokey quartz to the setting sun.

I invite the unseen to speak. So many dead,
it's said Confederates were left to rot.
In war, not all bodies are returned home
nor graves marked. I google "Mexicans
in the Civil War" and uncover layers
to the Treaty of Guadalupe Hidalgo
and Cinco de Mayo. This is how I meet
ancestors for the first time, heroes

this country decorates in clownish sombreros
and fake mustaches, dishonors for fighting
European empire on shared American land
Power & Money dictate can't be shared.
Years before this, carrying water gallons
up an Arizona mountain ridge to replenish
supplies in a pass known as "Dead Man's,"
I wrote messages on bottles to the living,

scanned Sonoran canyons for the lost,
and knew too many would not be found.
A black Sharpie Virgen drawn on hot plastic
became a prayer: may the next officer halt
before cracking her face beneath his boot,
spilling life on to dirt. No, nothing's funny
when you're brown in a country you're taught
isn't yours, your dead don't count.

THREE

"Let me call it, *a garden.*"

- Natalie Diaz, "From the Desire Field"

Seeking Sunday Morning Guitar Riffs

Play me a song, & I'll dance.
Write me a song, & I'm yours.

The swallowtail's proboscises curl
atop its head in a crown. I work

to be just as natural. I unfurl
my tongue. Drink you in. Call

your toxins self-preservation.
White nectar trickles down my chin,

on to my belly, keeps me shimmering.
Bitterness breaks into bright orange

spots atop iridescent blue wings,
makes a scene. You magic me

into song, & I'm platinum
in partygoers' ears playing on & on.

She Is Me, but We Are We

After John & Yoko's Bed-Ins for Peace

Forget what they say about suns and sunsets.
The key is *together. We can get it together. We
can* smooth fresh ivory sheets across a king,

arrange sugar chrysanthemums in bountiful
bouquets about the bed. You'll tune a favorite guitar,
the hand-me-down that fits right in your lap, fluff

a pillow for her to sit. Don't be afraid to call her
love, or the rectangle floating in the room: *island*,
beginning, *great society*. She won't be afraid

to pen a philosophy about your hands, the way
they finger frets and stroke strings when she
requests a song, which she only does when necessary.

Together we can invite the children, welcome picture
books and teddy bears, elect Mr. Bear queen, allow them
to appoint a family chancellor. Together we can

watch jaded edges lose teeth and listen to voices pouring
like cream when songs are about peace, or moons,
or roses, or any fucking cliché we can think to sing.

Mother Days

Mariachi trumpets blared, and Mom
threw a grito from deep inside her belly.
Life praise and death cry pulsated
from her throat like a gift from ancestors

while papel picado calaveras partied
along pink walls. Flowers sprouted
from tabletops and girls' heads,
and grandchildren dance-played viejitos.

On the cake, la Catrina, dressed in purple
frosting, mimicked mom's smirk
as if to say, *Not so fast!* But that
was another age, a 70th celebration.

Today la Doña is in bed and deflated
of hot air. Her instrument works overtime
to heal a broken femur, to intertwine cells
with a metal rod, make her music again.

It's Mother's Day. She cries for her suegra,
and not her mother. "She always
made my favorite food," she whimpers,
imagining bowls of espinazo en mole.

"My mom didn't even care to— "
She needs help calling forth a woman's spirit.
Like a butterfly, it flutters just beyond this
bedroom window, this borrowed hospital bed.

Grandma once taught me hospital beds
are for kissing death, but now her lesson
is patience. Together we wait for mothers
and daughters to return to trumpets.

On This Page

I scratch fears from your pandemic beard, wipe the year from your face, thumb the white stripe mourning down your chin, leave long kisses on your cheek, and when you say, *longer*, leave another without hesitation, without wondering how much time we have till she comes, or if you'll invite me in.

On the white of this page my love has all day and many rooms to roam. Comfort lounges slow and naked. I lay my body across a bed for you, down onto the floor, in front of a fire. I serve it on a platter, and you lift the oyster to your lips, lap its pearl in luster. I grow

more precious. I'm a coral reef, and you move careful, study tides. I'm an old house on the Pacific, and you ask to visit. I say *stay*, and you say *yes*. Outside our windows, birds sing along to a tune you pluck on guitar as we attempt an imperfect harmony.

On the confines of this space, I cast in circles. Caught in my own nets, love panics. You say your scent is wood floor, and my nose burns. Let the spell be folding this paper, offering it to waves, and asking ocean to swallow. Let the magic be forgiveness for when the ritual repeats, and when it's complete.

The Poet's Corrido

After Frida Kahlo's *The Dream (The Bed)*

"I had the strangest dream," she says not asking
permission to continue. "I'm in my bed,
but it's not my bed." This is how all dream retellings
begin. "I'm flying through the sky!" She means

floating in clouds. She does not yet have the word
for *tree* or for how it entombs her body in leaves.
Death is in the dream, but she won't name him.
His femurs are bound by explosives. She's losing

time and decides her marigold blanket is "a gold cape
weaved for a warrior." She writes *lavender lilies*
on a piece of parchment. But the ticking still ticks.
Details mix. "Sharks hunt the heavens!" From bed,

she pens *door handle, knock, unlock.* Open
possibility for the poet sprouting roots from toes.

Rancherita

Tengo panza. No
panzita, pero panzota.
And cypress thighs,
brown and strong,
that cling to your cliffs
reminding you
you're not yet ocean.
Lucky you to have
earth's devotion,
to be gripped tight
by beginnings.
This rancherita belongs
beyond borders,
grows over and under
fences, wild. Untamable
is not unattainable. She is
mountain woman.
Nopalita with spines.
A jumping cholla,
a chola that jumps
at the first sign of hate.
Wait. I can't claim chola.
I've never been honored
a hood name, but her hoops
rock with the spine within.

I'm Not Your Torta

These buns
are not for your
hands to grab. Don't
even think of bearing your
mouth to this deliciousness. You
don't know how to eat a torta right,
meaning you don't love it, meaning
you can't appreciate its rolls or how
grease runs hot down your chin. Too
many times you left me cold. But
Grandma taught me love as a
barehand flipping tortillas,
fingertips burning
con ganas.

Variations on a Wooden Spoon

I spoon-feed you sweetness
when you're weak & overworked.

I don't mind as long as you spoon
me in the soft glow of dawn,

yellow light on the skin of dreams.
Skin to skin is how I'm nourished,

how bones & heart grow strong.
Let me grip your long, hard handle

& lead you to my mouth like a plane
or train. No, let you come all man.

Let the dark tip of you soak in
steaming parts of me. Let it stir & stay

so long we swell & warp. Simply put,
let us fit into the other & never starve.

Conversation with the Heart

Los Angeles, August 2020

At dawn, the sun is a red pill and my heart,
a sealed pistachio. I lay in bed, feeling

for an opening, something to savor. Nothing
but battery acid on the tongue. Crystalized eyes

pain to shut. I pull away to examine
boarded-up chambers alone. A snoring hand

draws me back by the waist. I want this
to ease, but his touch freezes.

You've been too quick to pick apart his words.
The heart speaks. *You slice your mother's words*

like onions and refuse to cry. It's not my fault!
Smoked skies taste of ash, and I miss

the color green, the scent of day. I place
his hand in the rind of my chest. Ask to fruit.

What Was Meant to Be

After Eternal Sunshine of the Spotless Mind

A murder of bullies menaces the boy
into hammering a dead bird. He's cloaked
in a red cape. The girl finds him there.
She's crowned in a pink cowboy hat
and reaches for his hand.
He wants to stand up to the boys,
but she says it's not worth it.
"They're not. Worth it."

Still, they were always meant to break up.

You and I were never meant for more than
a waxing moon. But the fullness of your kiss
still glows brilliant.

You shared your Coke with me.
Took me dancing. Spun me at a concert
in the park on a cool summer night.
You couldn't believe
no one else had ever spun me.
True and not true. There was always
my mother. But this.
This was different. Wasn't it.

Afterward, you grew mean in the street.
I shrank small. Still.

If we stop right now, grab our belongings,
and exit the vehicle, that can't erase the laugh-scream
that bellowed from my body as we chased a track
spinning fast around a mountain. The path
was always set. The ride was always meant to be
exhilarating.

When I was little, perfect braids tugged at
the crown of my head and every worry that said
to not be a bother. I imagine your wild
curls couldn't quite cape ears
from harsh words that said you
weren't enough. But for a moment.
We reached for the other's hand.
Worth it.

The Way Men Use Me

They tell me
I'm their ideal
body type and I'm better
than *Pornhub*.
They seek out women
like me, big asses and curly hair,
but they can't quite find
satisfaction. Pobrecitos.
I know. They tell me.

They say, "I need you,"
and "You're the best
distraction." They say, "Later."
And then, "Later." And again,
"Later." They mean, *Never*.
"Plans changed"
is the tattered towel they toss over
my birdcage heart.

But when their need comes
all dripping teeth—
under or over me—
oh, how grunts say they're fooling
the devil, fronting
the self, fucking
death into oblivion, or so,
they think.

And when they call me
"muse," I know they mean *comfort*.
And when I plea, "Take me
to flower gaze
and you can gaze at me
all you want,"
we never do see the rainbowed tulips
in spring. Still, I know,
they, too, have their season.

Sanctuary

As they become known to and accepted by us, our feelings and the honest exploration of them become sanctuaries and spawning grounds for the most radical and daring ideas.

- Audre Lorde, "Poetry is Not a Luxury"

I tell a man straight for the first time, "I need to be valued," and a hot pink tropical flower blooms. I step back to see the many retaining walls I've built. I recognize these as fears, and vines grow and stretch until every border is reclaimed. As the garden becomes more lush, more green, so, too, my voice becomes more rich. Soon call outs echo through the valley, and each one becomes a tree to sit under and rest. I put my hand to a knot in a thick trunk of an oak and ask her to hold me. Trees are homes that need caring. Their roofs need fixing. To speak truth is upkeep. I welcome others to sit under trees, to bring their blankets and their poems.

We call it a mitote and wear magnolias in our hair. Like ears, their magenta petals are best suited for holding our tears. Our screams are the fertile soil holding the bones of every woman's scream that came before us. Our breath and saliva feed the hills we raise together. The hills our nieces and daughters climb to paint birds, be an ocean.

Ritual of Wholeness

Yellow lemons grew ripe
behind her house,
and when I was younger,
but no longer little,
I would speed past her
working in the kitchen, barely
a hello, out the back door,
to select a single, bright Myer.
Grandma stayed silent
as I carried the fruit in, laid it
at the counter, bared the knife,
sliced it through the belly.
Not until we were seated
at the table, she watching
from across the way
as I squeezed and spilled juice
over a bowl of tender frijoles
swimming in caldo, not until
I devoured two healthy helpings,
did she say with a wink,
"¿Porqué no comes? ¿No tienes
hambre?" As if to say, want
could never be shameful.

NOTES ON POEMS

<u>ONE</u>
"The Mermaid Game": This poem is dedicated to the 21 students and teachers who lost their lives on May 24, 2022 in a mass shooting at Robb Elementary in Uvalde, Texas. It's been widely reported that two of those murdered, Annabell Guadalupe Rodríguez (10) and Xavier López (10), would text each other "I love you" every night before bed. This poem is in remembrance of their love.

"Jack and Jill": This poem is in response to a photo submitted by Hazel Kight Witham of her two children running up a hill in the Bellona Wetlands Ecological Preserve. She is also an LAUSD teacher who took part in the UTLA strikes in January 2019. This poem is one of thirty I wrote in April 2020 for National Poetry Month. A poem-a-day project, I wrote love poems to friends based on their submitted photos and published both the photo and poem on my Instagram @xochitljulisa. Poems marked with a date from April 2020 were part of this series.

"Ursa Minor": This poem is in response to "The Stars Above Me," by Charity Capili Ellis (@ccapelliscreate). Both print and poem were exhibited in the collaborative art show, *The Broadside Project*, curated by Jessica Ceballos y Campbell and Sergio Teran at Avenue 50 Studio in September 2019.

"Mamita, We're Going on Ahead": Claudia Patricia Gómez González was a 19-year-old Guatemalan woman who was shot and killed by Border Patrol May 23, 2018. In the *New York Times* article, "'Don't Treat Us Like Animals': Family of Woman Shot by Border Patrol Denounces U.S." (May 26, 2018), it's reported her mother, Lidia González Vásquez recalled her daughter telling her when she left, "Mamita, we're going to go on ahead."

"The Hustle or What We Call Work": This poem is dedicated to Salvadorean American, Andrés Guardado. He was shot in the back by Compton Police on June 18, 2020 at 18 years old. His family maintains he was working as a security guard at the time of his murder. Law enforcement refutes this claim noting he was too young to be licensed for the job.

"For the Love of Home": A first draft of this poem was written for the collaborative video poem, "For the Love of L.A.," directed by photographer, Rafael Cardenas (@rafa.la). The original poem imagined knocking down the belltower of the San Gabriel Mission, a 250-year-old site of colonialism and white supremacy in my hometown and my family's church. On July 11, 2020, a fire destroyed the mission's roof. This caused me to rewrite the poem and to reconsider the meaning of *dismantle*.

TWO
First drafts of these poems were written while in residence at the Gettysburg National Military Park as the "Poet in the Parks" from September 15, 2017-October 7, 2017. During these three weeks, NFL protests and the Las Vegas mass shooting were major news stories, as well as the ongoing debates over Civil War monuments, reignited by the Charlottesville protests and the murder of Heather D. Heyer on August 12, 2017 by a white supremacist.

"Living with the Dead": The 11th Massachusetts Infantry Monument at the Gettysburg National Military Park is inscribed with following Shakespeare quote: *"All's well that ends well."* For images and details on this monument as well as other monuments at this site (there are over 1,000), visit gettsyburg.stonesentinels.com.

"Self-Portrait of Expectation": This poem is inspired by the poetry collection *When I Grow Up I Want to be a List of Further Possibilities* by Chen Chen and his series of self-portraits.

"Caballito del Diablo: What Does Not Disappear": This poem is inspired by the book *Antígona González* by Sara Uribe. On page 66 Uribe writes, "Un caballito del diablo frente a lo que desaparece. Frente a lo que desaparece. : Frente a lo desaparece: lo que no desaparece." On 67 the English translation by John Pluecker reads, "A dragonfly facing what disappears. Facing what disappears. : Facing what disappears: what does not disappear."

THREE
"She Is Me, but We Are We": In 1969 John Lennon and Yoko Ono used the event of their honeymoon to stage a protest of the war in Vietnam. For two weeks they stayed in bed to "Make love. Not war." Journalists were invited to conduct interviews and record their protest. In one recorded conversation, John Lennon is seen on the phone passionately telling someone, "Together. We can get it together. We can get it together. Now that's all."

"I'm Not Your Torta": a "torta" is a derogatory word for woman regularly referenced on the *Foos Gone Wild* Instagram account.

"Conversation with the Heart": During August 2020 California was experiencing the "August wildfire siege." An unprecedented 650 wildfires ignited across the state making the air quality extremely dangerous, and before Covid vaccines were released, this meant gathering outside was nearly impossible.

"Sanctuary": March 7, 2020 #DignidadLiteraria organizers hosted a Read-in & Mitote at AWP San Antonio. Over 50 Latinx poets and writers were invited to sit on blankets in a public square and read from their books. We were protesting the whitewashing of Latinx stories and characters in literary publishing. My use of the word *mitote* is in remembrance of this protest.

PAGES 29-30 ENDNOTES

1. Most literary journals say posting a poem on social media is publication and makes it ineligible for publication with them. As director of Women Who Submit, I made a practice of advising new poets to follow this guideline, but since the chaos of 2020, my practice has changed. The poem titled "Why I'll Never Again Advise Poets Against Publishing on Social Media" is in response to online publication.

2. When this poem was first published at *womenwhosubmitlit.org* on July 8, 2020, the number of deaths was 130,000. The final revision of this poem was made in April 2023. On April 4, 2023 the number was 1,125,366. (https://covid.cdc.gov)

3. Sandra Bland was a 28 year-old #blacklivesmatter activist who addressed police violence and racism in a Facebook video series she called "Sandy Speaks." In an April 8, 2015 video, she says: "In the news that we've seen as of late, you can stand there, surrender to the cops, and still be killed." (https://www.youtube.com/watch?v=ClKeZgC8lQ4)

4. In the Treaty of 1868, the US Government promised the Lakota territory that included the Black Hills—and Tȟuŋkášila Šákpe, a sacred mountain also known as the Six Grandfathers—in order to squash fighting, but when gold was discovered in the next decade, the US confiscated the land. Fighting continued until the massacre at Wounded Knee in 1890 where "hundreds of unarmed Sioux women, children, and men were shot and killed by U.S. troops." In 1927 Tȟuŋkášila Šákpe was dynamited for a sculpture of four American Presidents. (https://www.pbs.org/wgbh/americanexperience/features/rushmore-sioux/)

5. The Standing Rock Sioux Tribe began fighting against the building of the Dakota Access Pipeline in early 2016. #NoDAPL protests first gained national attention through social media in April 2016. May 20, 2021, Judge James Boasberg, "allowed the controversial Dakota Access Pipeline to continue operating" while an impact report was being conducted. In February 2022, The Standing Rock Sioux Tribe withdrew as a cooperating agency from the completion this impact report. For more on why they withdrew and how to get involved, visit the Standing Rock Sioux Tribe website. (https://standingrock.org/dapl-eis/)

6. Flint's water crisis began on April 25, 2014 when the city switched its water source endangering the residents of Flint, a majority-Black city, with lead poisoning and lead poisoning-related health risks. According to the January 17, 2023 ABC News story, "Flint residents urged to filter water as bottled water donations end amid ongoing water crisis," "The residential lead service line replacement was initially set to be finished in 2019, according to a settlement agreement with the city. That deadline was eventually pushed back to the fall of 2022 and has most recently been set for completion in August 2023, according to city officials." (https://abcnews.go.com/US/flint-residents-urged-filter-water-bottled-water-donations/story?id=96531880)

ACKNOWLEDGEMENTS

Thank you to the editors of the following publications in which poems from this collection, sometimes in earlier versions, appeared:

Academy of American Poets' *Poem-a-Day*
Acentos Review
Board of Photography
Cutthroat's *Puro Chicanx Writers Anthology*
A Dozen Nothing
Exposition Review
Huizache
The Music Center's *For the Love of L.A.*
On Being's *Poetry Unbound*
Poetry Unbound: 50 Poems to Open Your World (W.W. Norton)
Santa Fe Writers Project
Sin Cesar (formerly *Dryland Lit*)
The Texas Review
VIBE: Violet Indigo Blue, Etc.
Voices de la Luna

Thank you to the December 2019 A-B Projects "The Stacks" art exhibition curated by Andy Anderegg, A-B Projects Director, Nicole Seisler, Stanton Hunter, Los Angeles Print Shop, and Esteban Pulido for the publication and exhibition of my chapbook, *Locating the Dead: The Gettysburg Poems.*

Thank you to the Gettysburg National Military Park, National Parks Arts Foundation, and the Poetry Foundation for my "Poet in the Park" fellowship in September 2017. Thank you to Dorland Arts for giving me a space to revise in April 2021.

A special thank you to Rafael Cardenas for inviting me to write a poem for The Music Center's "For the Love of L.A." video poem series in partnership with Self-Help Graphics. To Ching-in Chen for inviting me to submit a poem for *The Texas Review* in 2017. At that time, I was being eaten by anxiety, but thanks to Ching-in, I had an opportunity to try again. And to Maria Maloney for first publishing one of my poems in 2009 and supporting my work along the way.

Thank you to Hazel Kight Witham, Ryane Nicole Granados, and Maggie Hayes (and everyone else whose poems didn't make it into the collection) for submitting photos on Instagram and allowing me to write you a love poem.

Thank you to those who gave me notes, inspiration, advice, and encouragement namely F. Douglas Brown, Noriko Nakada, Tisha Marie Reichle-Aguilera, Luivette Resto, Lauren Eggert-Crowe, Désirée Zamorano, Lisa Cheby, Bonnie Kaplan, Kat Kambes, Rocío Carlos, Vickie Vértiz, Melissa Bennet, Viktoria Valenzuela, Karla Cordero, Yaccaira Salvatierra, Kate Maruyama, and Jessica Ceballos y Campbell.

Lastly, I thank my family for always believing in me and being my biggest supporters. Dad, Mom, Vivien, Gabriel, Andrés, Raquel, Gabrielito, Armando, Paola, and Aurora, I love you.

AUTHOR'S BIOGRAPHY

Xochitl-Julisa Bermejo is the daughter of Mexican immigrants. A former Steinbeck Fellow and *Poets & Writers* California Writers Exchange winner, she's received residencies from Hedgebrook, Ragdale, Yefe Nof, and the National Parks Arts Foundation in partnership with Gettysburg National Military Park and the Poetry Foundation. She is the author of *Posada: Offerings of Witness and Refuge* (Sundress Publications). Her poem "Battlegrounds" was featured at Academy of American Poets' *Poem-a-Day,* On Being's *Poetry Unbound*, and the anthology, *Poetry Unbound: 50 Poems to Open Your World* (W.W. Norton). Her poetry can be found at *Acentos Review, Huizache, Santa Fe Writers Project*, and other journals. She teaches poetry and creative writing with Antioch University, MFA and UCLA Extension and is the director of Women Who Submit, a nonprofit organization empowering woman-identifying and nonbinary writers to submit work for literary publication. Inspired by her Chicana identity, she works to cultivate love and comfort in chaotic times.

Printed in the USA
CPSIA information can be obtained
at www.ICGtesting.com
LVHW052357051023
760147LV00009B/184

9 781957 840215